ALSO BY MARY BUFFETT AND DAVID CLARK

Buffettology

The Buffettology Workbook

The New Buffettology

The Tao of Warren Buffett

*Warren Buffett and the Interpretation
of Financial Statements*

WARREN BUFFETT'S
MANAGEMENT
SECRETS

Proven Tools for Personal and Business Success

MARY BUFFETT & DAVID CLARK

Scribner

NEW YORK LONDON TORONTO SYDNEY

SCRIBNER

A Division of Simon & Schuster, Inc.

1230 Avenue of the Americas

New York, NY 10020

First Scribner hardcover edition December 2009

SCRIBNER and design are registered trademarks of The Gale Group, Inc., used under license by Simon & Schuster, Inc., the publisher of this work.

For information about special discounts for bulk purchases, please contact Simon & Schuster Special Sales at 1-866-506-1949 or business@simonandschuster.com.

The Simon & Schuster Speakers Bureau can bring authors to your live event. For more information or to book an event contact the Simon & Schuster Speakers Bureau at 1-866-248-3049 or visit our website at www.simonspeakers.com.

Manufactured in the United States of America

1   3   5   7   9   10   8   6   4   2

Library of Congress Cataloging-in-Publication Data is available.

ISBN 978-1-4391-4937-9
ISBN 978-1-4391-5488-5 (ebook)

For Sam and Dexter

CONTENTS

STEP ONE

PICK THE RIGHT BUSINESS TO WORK FOR

STEP TWO

DELEGATE

STEP THREE

FIND THE RIGHT MANAGER FOR THE JOB

STEP FOUR

MOTIVATE YOUR WORKFORCE

STEP FIVE

MANAGERIAL PITFALLS, CHALLENGES, AND LEARNING OPPORTUNITIES

INTRODUCTION

In the chronicles of the investment life of Warren Buffett much has been written about his investment methods. Each and every investment he has ever made has been taken apart and analyzed in excruciating detail. David and I alone have written the books *Buffettology, The Buffettology Workbook, The New Buffettology, The Tao of Warren Buffett,* and *Warren Buffett and the Interpretation of Financial Statements*—all on Warren's investment methods and all international best-sellers.

But what was sorely missing from the body of Warren Buffett literature was a book that addresses and discusses the brilliant way Warren has managed his life, his businesses, and the people who manage Berkshire Hathaway's 233,000 employees around the globe. Besides being a genius at investing, Warren Buffett is also a genius of a manager, with over eighty-eight CEOs of different companies reporting directly or indirectly to him. In modern business no man has managed a more highly talented group of managers, in so many diverse businesses, and delivered such spectacular results.

In many ways Buffett's managerial record surpasses even

his amazing investment record with Berkshire Hathaway, where *the company's operational annual net income* grew from $18 a share in 1979 to $4,093 a share in 2007. This equates to a compounding annual growth rate of 21.39 percent, a record that indicates that Warren and his managers are doing a fantastic job of minding the store. (In comparison, *Berkshire's investment portfolio* for the same period grew at an annual compounding rate of 19.78 percent, which means we can argue that as a manager Warren outperformed himself as an investor.)

In our quest to bring you all things Warren Buffett, we have written the first ever book that takes an in-depth look at Warren's management methods—what they are, how they work, and how you can use them. We discuss the impact that Dale Carnegie had on Warren's life and how Carnegie's teachings helped transform Warren into the master manager he is today.

We have kept the book easy to read, with short chapters. The methods that Warren uses are simple and easy to understand, but, as you will see, their impact is powerful.

We look to the future and imagine many generations using Warren's enlightened management methods to inspire and motivate people of all ages to achieve their dreams and visions.

MARY BUFFETT AND DAVID CLARK
JULY 1, 2009

OVERVIEW

Warren Buffett's Management Secrets

Once upon a time there was a slightly nerdish young man by the name of Warren Buffett, who, at the age of twenty, was frightened to death to stand up in front of people and speak to them. Then he discovered Dale Carnegie's course on public speaking and it changed his life. Not only did he develop the courage and skill to speak in front of groups of people, he learned how to make friends and motivate people. Warren considers his Carnegie education a life-changing event and the most important diploma he has ever received.

Once Warren was comfortable with public speaking, he also became a devotee of Dale's philosophy on interacting with people. He read and reread Carnegie's book *How to Win Friends and Influence People* dozens of times, under-lining it and memorizing entire passages. The book became his bible for dealing with people and one of the cornerstones of his management philosophy.

Was he successful?

Here is what A. L. Ueltschi, the founder and chairman of

FlightSafety International Inc., the world's leading aviation training company, told author Robert P. Miles about Warren as his boss: "Leadership is really what a good manager is about. The letters of the word represent the qualities that a good manager should have:

L is for loyalty and
E is for enthusiasm.
A stands for attitude, and
D is for discipline.
E stands for example—you have to set a good example—and
R is for respect.
S represents scholarliness, and
H is for honesty.
I and
P stand for integrity and pride.

"The thing I like best about Warren Buffett is that he possess all these qualities."

We will examine Warren's leadership qualities and how Warren synthesized what he learned into a winning management formula, and became not only the manager that other managers want to emulate, but also the second richest man in the world.

To facilitate the learning process, we've broken down Warren's management philosophy into the following five segments or steps—each working with the others to create the perfect combination of management skills.

1. Pick the Right Business

Warren has figured out that not all businesses are created equal. The first step to success is to own, manage, or work for the right business with the right economics working in its favor. That's how to get ahead of the game right from the start, whether you are an owner, a manager, or an employee.

2. Delegate Authority

The second step is Warren's unique view on delegating authority, which has allowed him to grow Berkshire Hathaway from a small, failing textile company into a giant multinational conglomerate.

3. Find a Manager with the Right Qualities

The third step is to know the qualities that are needed to manage an excellent business—here Warren is looking for integrity, intelligence, and a passion for the business, which also happen to be the qualities that we need to cultivate in ourselves to be successful managers.

4. MOTIVATE YOUR WORKFORCE

Once the excellent business is found and the right manager is put into place, Warren has the job of motivating his managers to be all that they can be, so that the business, the manager, and the employees can be as productive as possible. Here we will spend time studying Warren's adaptation and expansion of Carnegie's methods. If there is a single skill that a manager should be great at, it is motivating others to achieve. Warren developed a specific set of motivational skills that have inspired his managers to hit one business home run after another and helped him build Berkshire Hathaway into the $150 billion market cap company that it is today.

5. MANAGERIAL AXIOMS FOR DIFFERENT PROBLEMS

And finally there are a number of specific Buffett managerial axioms for dealing with everything from managing leverage, to handling dishonest employees, to keeping costs low.

At the end of the book we will discuss a few "Warrenisms" that will help you manage your day-to-day life. Success in business and life usually go hand in hand, and Warren has some helpful hints that will help us improve our life management skills.

So without further ado . . .

WARREN BUFFETT'S
MANAGEMENT SECRETS

PICK
THE RIGHT BUSINESS
TO WORK FOR

Working for the right business can mean the difference between a successful, high-paying career or a life of drudgery. It can also mean the difference between a successful long-term investment and one that earns nothing. Warren has discovered that certain kinds of companies have inherent business economics so great that even a bad manager will look good working for them. These are the companies that he wants to own, and these are the kinds of companies that we want to work for. Warren has identified a number of characteristics to help us identify these wonderful businesses, which is where we will begin.

CHAPTER 1

How to Find the Kind of Business That Offers the Greatest Career Opportunities

"There is a huge difference between the business that grows and requires lots of capital to do so and the business that grows and doesn't require capital."

—WARREN BUFFETT

This is one of the keys to understanding Warren's success as a long-term investor and business manager. Businesses with superior economics working in their favor tend to burn considerably less capital than they earn. This is usually because they produce a brand-name product that never has to change, or because they provide a key service that allows them to charge higher prices, which gives them better profit margins.

With a brand-name product that never has to change, the company doesn't have to spend large sums of money on research and development, nor does it have to constantly retool its plant and equipment to implement design changes. Therefore, it can use the same plant and equipment over and over again, year after year, until the equipment finally wears out. All the money it saves can be used to expand the business without having to burden the company with additional debt or the selling of new shares. The capital needed for growth is generated internally. All of this, of course, helps make the managers of these super companies look brilliant!

An example: A company like Coca-Cola never has to spend billions of dollars redesigning its product or retooling its manufacturing plants to stay ahead of the competition. This leaves it plenty of money to spend on such fun things as buying other companies and paying big bonuses to its managers. A company like General Motors, on the other hand, which produces automobiles that change in style almost every year, has to spend billions on new designs and retooling its plants to keep its models competitive with the Fords and Toyotas of the world.

Which one of these companies would you rather work for—the one that is internally generating tons of excess cash or the one that is internally burning tons of cash? The one with the excess cash, of course, because that excess cash makes management look good, which means that they get to pay themselves generous bonuses at the end of the year.

And getting paid more money is always a good thing.

Companies with a Durable Competitive Advantage

Warren believes that the best company to own, invest in, or work for—the one that offers the greatest opportunity for career advancement, job security, and the long-term making of money—is a company that has what Warren calls a durable competitive advantage. These super companies have a near lockdown on their market. What this means to us is that these companies have products and services that never really change, are easy to sell, and own a piece of the consumer's mind. This equates to higher profit margins and inventory turnover, which means these companies are often awash in cash.

On the other side of the coin, there are companies with lousy economics that are very difficult businesses for us ever to look good in. They tend toward boom-and-bust cycles that make you a star one moment and out of a job the next.

So the businesses that offer us the greatest employment advantage are the ones with some kind of durable competitive advantage working in their favor. Warren has figured out that these super companies come in three basic business models: They either (1) sell a unique product, (2) sell a unique service, or (3) are the low-cost buyer and seller of a product or service that the public is consistently in need of.

Let's take a good look at each of these three kinds of

super businesses and discover the employment opportunities that they offer.

Companies that sell a unique product: This is the world of Coca-Cola, Pepsi, Wrigley, Hershey, Coors, Guinness, Kraft, Merck & Company, Johnson & Johnson, Procter & Gamble, and Philip Morris. Through the process of customer need and experience, and promotion by advertising, these companies have established the stories of their products in our minds and we immediately think of their products when we go to satisfy a specific need. Want to chew some gum? You might think of Wrigley. Feel like having a cold beer after a hot day on the job? You might think of Budweiser or Coors. For the last 284 years the Irish, on cool rainy evenings, have thought of pints of Guinness and a warm fire at the local pub. And Philip Morris has made a fortune selling Marlboro cigarettes all over the world.

Warren likes to think of these companies as owning a piece of the consumer's mind, and when a company owns a piece of the consumer's mind it never has to change its products, which, as you will find out, is a good thing. And it also gets to charge higher prices and sell more of its products, which means bigger profit margins and higher inventory turnover, which equates to a larger bottom line on its income statement. These companies are easy to identify because they have consistent and strong yearly earnings, and little or no debt on their balance sheets.

From an employment perspective, these special companies offer us the easiest opportunity to rise to managerial superstardom. They are awash in cash, which means that they can pay generous salaries and huge bonuses, and they also have the money to buy other businesses and create new businesses, which means that there is plenty of opportunity for a young manager to excel. Believe it or not, things really do go better with a Coke, including your career.

Companies that sell a unique service: This is the world of Moody's, H&R Block, Amex, ServiceMaster, and Wells Fargo. Like lawyers and doctors, these companies sell services that people need and are willing to pay for—but unlike lawyer and doctors, these companies are institutional specific as opposed to people specific. When you think of getting your taxes done you think of H&R Block, you don't think of Jack, the guy at H&R Block who does your taxes. The economics of selling a unique service can be phenomenal. A company doesn't have to spend a lot of money on redesigning its products, nor does it have to spend a fortune building a production plant and warehousing its wares. And firms selling unique services that own a piece of the consumer's mind can produce even better margins than firms selling products. Being a manager in one of these businesses can be a high-paying, rewarding career, with few of the financial ups and downs that plague other businesses. Just compare the operations histories of H&R Block and a company like GM. No matter how bad the recession, people still need help filing their taxes—there is never a recession in the tax-filing business. But with a company like GM the whims of the economy can be devastating in just a short amount of time. The management team of H&R Block will never stay awake nights worrying about union demands, too much debt, or the buying whims of the public. The same cannot be said for the management team of GM.

Companies that are the low-cost buyer and seller: This is the world of Wal-Mart, Costco, Nebraska Furniture Mart, Borsheim's Fine Jewelry, and the Burlington Northern Santa Fe. Here big margins are traded for volume, with the increase in volume more than making up for the decrease in profit margins. The key here is to be the low-cost buyer, which allows you to get your margins higher than your competitors' and still be the low-cost seller of a product or service. Here the reputation of being the best price in town lures in consumers.

In Omaha, if you need a new stove for your home, you go to the Nebraska Furniture Mart for the best selection and the best price. Want to ship your goods cross-country? The Burlington Northern can give you the best deal for your money. Live in a small town and want the best selection with the best prices? You go to Wal-Mart.

Out of the three business models just discussed, the low-cost buyer and seller offers the fewest opportunities for career advancement. The continued stress of having to keep costs low puts great pressure on management and tends to keep salaries low, yet these businesses still offer better employment and management opportunities than do the mediocre businesses that do not fit into one of these three categories.

Now that we know the general model for the "perfect" business to work for, let's look at their economic picture a little more closely so we can tell who is who and what companies are our tickets to that very rewarding career. We have selected three very simple economic tests to use to help determine if the company in question is one of those special companies with a durable competitive advantage.

CHAPTER 2

Three Quick Tests
for Identifying the Best Company
to Work For

1. PER-SHARE EARNINGS TEST

One of the quickest ways to check the economics of a potential employer is to check the company's yearly per-share earnings figures. This is easy to do if the company is a publicly traded entity, difficult to do if it is not.

While no one yearly per-share figure can be used to identify a company with a durable competitive advantage, per-share earnings for a ten-year period can give us a very clear picture of whether or not the company has a long-term competitive advantage working in its favor. What Warren looks for is a per-share earnings picture, over a ten-year period, that shows consistency and an upward trend.

Something that looks like this:

'08	$2.95
'07	$2.68
'06	$2.37
'05	$2.17
'04	$2.06
'03	$1.95
'02	$1.65
'01	$1.60
'00	$1.48
'99	$1.30

This shows Warren that the company has consistent earnings that are showing a long-term upward trend, which is an excellent sign that the company in question has some kind of long-term competitive advantage working in its favor and potentially would be a great company to work for. Consistent earnings are usually a sign that the company is selling a product or a mix of products that don't need to go through the expensive process of change. The upward trend in earnings means that the company's economics are strong enough to allow it either to make strategic expenditures to increase market share through advertising and an expansion in operations or to increase per-share earnings by the use of stock buy-backs.

The companies that Warren stays away from and that probably offer poor employment prospects have an erratic yearly earnings picture that looks like this:

'08	$2.50
'07	$(0.45) loss
'06	$3.89
'05	$(6.05) loss
'04	$6.39
'03	$5.03
'02	$3.35
'01	$(1.77) loss
'00	$(6.68) loss
'99	$8.53

This shows a downward trend, punctuated by losses, which tells Warren this company is in a fiercely competitive industry prone to booms and busts. The boom increases demand, which increases prices. To meet demand the company increases production, which increases supply, which increases costs and eventually leads to an excess of supply in the industry and to falling prices. The company, once profitable, now starts to lose money, until it has to cut production and costs. There are thousands of companies like this, and their erratic earnings, which in boom years create the illusion that the company is a winner, eventually make the company a loser. It is hard to look like a managerial superstar when every few years the company's inherently lousy economics destroy your results.

The company with consistent earnings that show an upward trend is the company that offers the best prospects for profitable long-term employment and a rewarding career. But the company with the erratic earnings picture, while quick to hire in the boom years, is also quick to fire in the lean years. This boom-and-bust pattern makes the company difficult to work for since there is no long-term stability in its economic picture.

2. THE DEBT TEST

Another sign of a great business to work for is a company with the absence of, or low levels of, long-term debt. Companies that make a lot of money don't need to carry high debt loads since the surplus of cash allows them to be self-financing. These are the companies that make good long-term employers because they have the cash to pay good salaries and the financial wherewithal to weather a recession with flying colors.

The no/low-debt companies are easy to spot, as long as you gauge the debt load of a particular business relative to its industry. As a general rule, a debt load in excess of five times its net earnings is a good indication that it is not a company with a durable competitive advantage.

High levels of debt tell us that: (1) the business is in a highly competitive industry where constant change has created high capital demands, or (2) the company is highly leveraged. What this means to us is that if we go to work for one of these businesses, the cost of servicing the debt will eat up any excess cash and leave little for salary increases and bonuses. It also means that there will be little excess capital for growing the business or acquiring new businesses, which means that there will be little growth in managerial opportunities. And if the economy goes into a recession, these will be the first companies that fire employees, in an attempt to cut costs before they go under. Not exactly the company that you want to be staking your career on.

3. The Gross Margin Test

Another way to tell if a company has a durable competitive advantage, which would help make it a great company to work for, is to look at the company's Gross Profit Margin. To figure out the company's Gross Profit Margin, we have to look at the company's Income Statement—which is a financial report for a period of time that shows whether the company made or lost money.

Specifically we have to take the company's Revenue and subtract the company's Cost of Goods Sold, which will give us the company's Gross Profit. Now, if we divide the company's Gross Profit by its Revenue, we will get the company's Gross Profit Margin. Let's take a closer look:

INCOME STATEMENT
Revenue	10, 000
Cost of Goods Sold	*-6,000*
Gross Profit	4,000

Now, if we subtract from the company's total revenue the amount reported as its Cost of Goods Sold, we get the company's reported Gross Profit. As an example: Total Revenue of $10 million less Cost of Goods Sold of $6 million, equals a Gross Profit of $4 million. Then, to get the Gross Profit Margin, we take the Gross Profit of $4,000 ÷ Revenue $10,000 = Gross Profit Margin, which equals 40%.

Warren is looking for companies that have some kind of durable competitive advantage—businesses that he can profit from over the long run—which make them fantastic companies to work for. What he has found is that companies that have excellent long-term economics working in their favor tend to have consistently higher Gross Profit Margins than those that don't. Let us show you:

Gross Profit Margin of companies that Warren has already

identified as having a durable competitive advantage: Coca-Cola shows a consistent Gross Profit Margin of 60% or better; the bond-rating company Moody's, 73%; the Burlington Northern Railroad, 61%; and the very chewable Wrigley Gum, 51%.

Contrast these excellent businesses with several companies that we know have poor long-term economics, such as the in-and-out-of-bankruptcy United Airlines, which shows a Gross Profit Margin of 14%; troubled automaker General Motors, which comes in at a weak 21%; the once-troubled but now-profitable U.S. Steel, at a not-so-strong 17%; and Goodyear Tire—which runs in any weather but a bad economy—stuck at a not-very-impressive 20%.

In the tech world—a field Warren stays away from because he doesn't understand it—Microsoft shows a consistent Gross Profit Margin of 79%, while Apple comes in at 33%. These numbers indicate that Microsoft produces better economics selling operating systems and software than Apple does selling hardware and services.

What creates a high Gross Profit Margin is the company's durable competitive advantage. It allows companies the freedom to price the products and services well in excess of their Cost of Goods Sold. Without a competitive advantage, companies have to compete by lowering the price of the product or service they are selling, which of course lowers their profit margins and therefore their profitability. It also lowers their ability to raise salaries and give big bonuses, and it diminishes the companies' capacity to expend capital on new businesses and to survive a recession.

In Summary

There are other tests that we can run to help us determine if the company in question has a durable competitive advantage, and we outline those tests in great detail in our book *Warren Buffett and the Interpretation of Financial Statements.* But for the quick and dirty, the three tests described in this chapter will serve us well when we need to assess whether or not the company offering us a job is one of those great businesses that will take us down the path to a successful and very rewarding career, or if it is a mediocre business that will enslave us to a life of low wages, few opportunities, and little or no job security.

While it is within the realm of possibility for a great company, over time, to turn into a mediocre one—this happened to the newspaper industry—it is a very rare event for a mediocre business to turn into a great one. So if you find yourself working for a company with poor inherent economics, it is better to get out now than to stick around year after year waiting for things to change.

DELEGATE

Warren discovered that as Berkshire grew larger and larger, and was involved in more and more diverse businesses, delegating authority became a necessity not only for his sanity, but to ensure that his companies were competently run and that the managers were happy running them. If there is a single management skill that is uniquely Warren, it is his willingness to delegate authority way beyond boundaries that most CEOs would be comfortable with. Let's explore Warren's philosophy on delegation and how it has allowed him to grow Berkshire from a small regional textile manufacturer into the giant multinational conglomerate that it has become today.

CHAPTER 3

Rules for Delegating Authority

"We delegate almost to the point of abdication."

— WARREN BUFFETT

Warren learned that to run and to grow a business, one must learn the art of delegating authority. The natural inclination is to try to control every event and the people involved; to micromanage the task, the venture, the business. But micromanaging too many tasks or businesses leads to too many balls in the air at once, and if you drop one, you drop them all. Micromanaging leads to neglect, whereas delegating to a competent manager who is focused on just one job means a more thorough understanding of the task, and a more careful execution of the job. Warren owns more than eighty-eight diverse businesses, and he has turned over the management of these companies to eighty-eight highly competent CEO managers. Berkshire companies like Johns Manville, Benjamin Moore, Fruit of the Loom, Clayton Homes, and Jordan's

Furniture are all run by CEOs who have complete control over their businesses. When Berkshire bought Forest River, Warren told its founder and CEO, Peter Liegl, not to expect to hear from him more than once a year. Warren even goes so far as to tell the CEOs of Berkshire's companies not to write up anything special for him. When McLane Company CEO Grady Rosier phoned him to request approval to buy a couple of new company jets, Warren replied, "That is your decision. It's your company to run."

Warren feels it would be sheer folly on his part to think that he could competently manage each and every one of these businesses himself. To get the job competently done, Warren delegates, not just a task, but the entire job. As he says, he delegates almost to the point of abdication.

Warren has developed a set of rules to help him delegate successfully:

RULE NO. 1

Every business culture is unique. From the smallest of firms to the largest of corporations, workers and managers have developed highly specialized skill sets that allow them to accomplish their tasks. As a manager, Warren has learned that he cannot perform these highly specialized skill sets even remotely as well as they can. He feels that his employees are the experts and should be allowed to do what they are good at doing without his interference. He also feels that if he has any job as a manager, it is to inspire his employees to greatness at their jobs. Think cheerleader, not slave driver.

Rule No. 2

Warren has discovered that competent managers like to be left alone to run "their" businesses as they see fit. Warren encourages his managers to continue to think of their businesses as their own. The result is they work harder and make sure that the business does well. For them it is a matter of pride.

Rule No. 3

Warren realizes that in order for complete delegation of authority to work, it is necessary not only that our managers be hard working, passionate, and intelligent about their businesses; they must also have a great deal of integrity. In other words, they must be as honest as the day is long. If they are not honest, they just may end up using their hard-working, passionate, and intelligent ways to rob us blind.

Warren's rules of delegation are fairly simple: Each and every business is unique. Your employees are better at doing their individual jobs than you are. If we want the business to grow, we must delegate authority. Managers like to be left alone to run "their businesses." And the managers we hire need to be hard working, intelligent, and, most important, honest. Or as the late, great Berkshire manager Mrs. B once said—regarding the secret to her success in the furniture business—"Sell cheap and tell the truth."

FIND THE RIGHT
MANAGER FOR THE JOB

O nce the right business is found or acquired, and the need for delegation understood, the next job is to hire the right manager for the job. For Warren, the characteristics of the right manager just happen to be the managerial qualities that we should cultivate in ourselves. Let's take a look at just what those characteristics are.

CHAPTER 4

Where Warren Starts His Search for the Right Manager

"Management changes, like marital changes, are painful, time consuming, and chancy."

—WARREN BUFFETT

T his is a lesson that Warren learned the hard way—by buying businesses that were available at a bargain purchase price but were poorly run. His early investment in Dempster Mills Manufacturing, which we will discuss in just a minute, is the perfect example of having to replace management several times before finding the right manager. Was this painful? Yes. Was it time consuming? Yes. Was it expensive? Very. Was it necessary? Most definitely.

The key to making managerial changes is to ask: Is it absolutely necessary? If the answer is no, we are out of our minds to risk financial ruin by bringing in someone completely new to take over. But if the business is losing money, and we think that that is due to the manager and not the underlying economics of the business, then it is definitely time for a change in management.

Warren tries to avoid managerial changes. When he advertises for new companies to buy, through investment bankers or his annual letter to Berkshire's shareholders, he insists that the businesses come with competent management already in place.

He requires the key managers of each of the companies he owns to write him a letter telling him who in the company would succeed them if they were to die tomorrow. These letters are updated each year. This way, if something does happen to one of his managers, time won't be wasted in trying to find a replacement. Warren gets a manager who is already familiar with the business and was hand-chosen by the person who best understood the company—its people, products, and customers.

If Warren has to look outside a company for a manager, he usually turns to people he has already worked with, who have a proven track record. Or he will ask his business associates for a recommendation. This brings us to the short but remarkable story of Dempster Mills Manufacturing and the remarkable Harry Bottle.

Dempster Mills Manufacturing was a windmill and water irrigation company in Nebraska that Warren bought into because the stock was selling at 25 percent of its book value. Once he had stock in the company and had taken a seat on its board of directors, he realized that the reason that the company wasn't doing very well was that it was poorly managed. So he convinced the board members to bring in a new manager—whom they chose. The new manager proved to be even more of a disaster than the manager they had replaced. In desperation, Warren turned to his friend and counsel Charlie Munger. He asked if Charlie knew of any managerial talent who could save the day. Charlie suggested the name of a man whom Warren would later refer to as "the remarkable Harry Bottle." Harry was what is known as a turnaround artist, a manager remarkably skilled at fixing failing businesses. At Warren's invitation and for a $50,000 signing bonus, Harry moved from warm, sunny California to bitterly cold Nebraska, where he stepped in as the new CEO of Dempster. The first thing Harry did was reprice the inventory of spare and replacement parts. Dempster's products needed constant upkeep, which meant that the company did a big business in replacement parts. Some of the parts that Dempster used could be bought at any hardware store, but some were unique to Dempster and couldn't be bought anywhere else. One of the errors that Harry discovered was that Dempster had been marking up all its parts at a standard 40 percent, both the common and unique ones. Harry tripled the price of the unique parts that Dempster had a monopoly on, and cut back on the inventory levels of the common parts, thereby increasing revenues and freeing up capital. By year's end, Dempster was back in the black and on its way to becoming one of Warren's winning investments.

Twenty years later, Warren had another managerial problem with one of Berkshire Hathaway's smaller manufacturing businesses, and guess who he called? The remarkable Harry Bottle, of course.

The lesson here is this: Change managers only when necessary, promote from within if possible, and if you can't, look for talent with a proven track record. When all else fails, call in the remarkable Harry Bottle.

CHAPTER 5

Victor or Victim? Warren's Secret
for Picking a Leader Out of the Pack

*"Would you rather be the world's greatest lover and have
everyone think that you are the world's worst lover? Or
would you rather be the world's worst lover and have
everyone think that you are the world's best lover?"*

—WARREN BUFFETT

Warren Buffett theorizes that all people have either an
inner or an outer scorecard: We are true to ourselves or we
conform to what we think the world wishes us to be. A true
leader follows the beat of his or her own drummer, while a
bureaucrat bends to the perceived wishes of others.

It is hard to stand alone when the winds of popular opinion are against you. Warren's ability to do this has made him
superrich. He buys stocks when everyone else is afraid, and
sells when everyone else is enthusiastic. He has spent his life

going against the herd. Free and independent thinkers like Warren Buffett are never victims. They are masters of their own destiny.

In discussing the difference between victor and victim mentality, psychologists talk about the locus of control. If you have an internal locus of control, you blame yourself when something goes wrong. You believe that you are in control of your fate and that you have control of the outcome, and if you fail, it's because of your own actions and no one else's. But if you have an external locus of control and something goes wrong, you blame everyone but yourself.

As a young man, Warren was deeply influenced by his father, Howard, who had a strong internal locus of control. When the Great Depression hit, Howard started a successful new business. When he disagreed with what was going on in government, he got himself elected to Congress. This taught Warren that he, not the world, was in control of his life and that he, not the world, would determine what his life would look like.

Having an internal locus of control is not always easy: When you win, it was you who won it, but when you lose, it was you who lost it. There is no scapegoat, no one other than yourself to blame, which can be crushing. Warren's failed investments in two Irish banks and his overpayment for ConocoPhillips are his failures and his alone, and he learned from them, but he makes a special point not to dwell on his failures for too long. By not dwelling on them, he avoids the crippling effects that failure can bring to someone with an internal locus of control.

The great lesson here is this: People with an internal locus of control take responsibility for their failures and in the process learn from their mistakes. They are in control of themselves; they are in control of their world. They see problems as challenges to be conquered. (Think Bill Gates.) People with an external locus of control don't believe that they have the power to solve their problems; they believe that they are the victims of circumstances that are beyond their control. (Think Wall Street.)

Which view do you think leads to riches and greatness? Which type of person would have the strength to lead a company or a nation through hard times? Are we victor or victim? Victors make great managers and leaders, because they can take responsibility and solve problems. Victims, on the other hand, are too busy inventing excuses and blaming the world to take up challenges and solve problems.

CHAPTER 6

Work at a Job You Love

"There comes a time when you ought to start doing what you want. Take a job that you love. You will jump out of bed in the morning. I think you are out of your mind if you keep taking jobs that you don't like because you think that it will look good on your résumé. Isn't that a little like saving up sex for your old age?"

—WARREN BUFFETT

In the quest for wealth, we often end up in jobs or professions that we don't like, but we stay at them day after day, year after year, until finally we have run out of time. We delude ourselves into believing that a day will come when we will finally do what we dream of doing. Meantime, we spend a life in misery, which we bring home with us each day to share with our loved ones. This type of suffering in the name of a buck usually starts early in life and is often predicated on need. However, sometimes its foundation is nothing more than greed. Warren believes that not doing what we love in the name of greed is very poor management of our lives. It makes work drudgery, which drags us down and destroys our spirit. And though we may be making a lot of money, the nine-plus hours we are at work we are miserable.

In the world of business, the people who are most successful are those who are doing what they love. Money isn't what drives them. What drives them is the same thing that drives a great ballplayer or a great musician: a love of what they do. Be it a computer programmer, a salesman, a carpenter, a nurse, a butcher, a chef, a policeman, a doctor, or a lawyer, the people who rise to the top are those who love what they do. And they are usually the people who make the most money in their profession. Loving what we do and earning good money almost always go hand in hand.

Warren believes that when we employ people to work for us, we must try to find people who are going to love what we hired them to do. These are the people who will take pride in their work, inspire their fellow workers to greatness, and become the driving force behind the business. They are also the people who have made men like Warren look like geniuses.

In the management of our lives, the rule is: Love what you do.

In the management of our businesses, the rule is: Hire people who love what they do.

Both will lead you to the gold.

CHAPTER 7

Put a Winning Sales Team Together

"I don't want to be on the other side of the table from the customer. I was never selling anything that I didn't believe in myself or use myself."

—WARREN BUFFETT

W arren learned early on that the best salespeople are those who believe in their products. Who have a passion for the products that they are selling.

If someone believes in and has a passion for the products he's selling, you can bet that he is very interested in everything about that product, from the materials it's made of to how it is manufactured, to what are its best uses. Even more important, this salesperson will know the best uses of the product. Such knowledge impresses any customer.

This is a quality that Warren is looking for in his managers—people who believe in their products and businesses so much that they love to go to work. He doesn't like hiring managers who are only interested in making money and who would rather be somewhere else. Many of Warren's top managers have spent the vast majority of their working lives at the same company and continue working for them even though they are millionaires many times over. Publisher Stan Lipsey of the *Buffalo News* has been with the company for over thirty years. CEO Irv Blumkin, now in his fifties, has been on the payroll of the Nebraska Furniture Mart since he was a teenager. Both of these super managers are wealthy enough to retire in the morning, but they keep showing up to work, and the reason? They love what they do.

The lesson here is this: If we want to put a winning sales team together, we must find people who believe in and are passionate about the products that we are asking them to sell. A salesman's passion for the products he is selling is something that Warren has learned he can bank on.

CHAPTER 8

Obsession

"Our prototype for occupational fervor is the Catholic tailor who used his small savings of many years to finance a pilgrimage to the Vatican. When he returned, his parish held a special meeting to get his firsthand account of the Pope. 'Tell us,' said the eager faithful, 'just what sort of fellow is he?' Our hero wasted no words. 'He's a forty-four medium.'"

—WARREN BUFFETT

In Warren's world the perfect manager is someone who gets up in the morning thinking about the business and at night is dreaming about the business. As he says, "Obsession is the price for perfection." Warren's obsession led him to memorize the Moody's stock manual, starting at A and working his way through to Z. One of his favorite all-time investors was a guy with very little education who became so obsessed with water companies that he could tell you how much money they made every time someone flushed the toilet. Guess what the guy made his millions investing in? Water companies, of course.

And it is obsession that Warren is looking for in his employees. He once said that if he could ask only one question of interviewees for a job at Berkshire it would be how obsessed they are with what they do. His archetype of the perfect manager was the famous Mrs. B, who started and managed the Nebraska Furniture Mart with her family until she reached the ripe old age of 104. There was no keeping the old girl away from the store, which was the love of her life. In the sixty-plus years she ran the business, she took only one vacation and was miserable the entire time because she was away from "her store." She said that when she went home at night she couldn't wait for morning so she could get back to "her customers." Her only hobby was driving around Omaha checking out the competition.

All of Warren's top managers are men and women obsessed. Tony Nicely, CEO of GEICO, has worked for the company since 1961 and has no idea what he would do if he ever retired.

Talking about A. L. Ueltschi, founder and chairman of FlightSafety, Warren said, "Al understood what I was about. I understood what FlightSafety was all about, and I could tell that he loved his business. The first question I always ask myself about somebody in his position is: Do they love the money or do they love the business? But with Al, the money is totally secondary. He loves the business and that's what I need, because the day after I buy a company, if they only love the money, they're gone."

A simple question that Warren uses to determine a manager's passion for the business is to find out about their early drive to be in business. He says that we can tell more about how successful a manager is going to be by whether or not he or she had a lemonade stand as a child than by where they went to college. An early love of being in business equates later in life to being successful in business.

In Warren's world it is not so much how smart we are as it is how obsessed we are, how much we love what we are doing. If we happen to be smart too, well, that is just icing on an obsessively delicious cake.

CHAPTER 9

The Power of Honesty

"We also believe candor benefits us as managers: The CEO who misleads others in public may eventually mislead himself in private."

—WARREN BUFFETT

Warren says that a manager or employee who is truthful with others about his mistakes is more likely to learn from them. When a manager or employee ignores his mistakes or is always trying to blame someone or something else for his own blunders, then he will more likely lie to himself about other important things as well.

Warren has found this to be especially true in matters of accounting and believes that a willingness to fuddle with one set of numbers will eventually lead to a willingness to misrepresent all the numbers. Or as Warren says, "Managers who always promise to 'make the numbers' will at some point be tempted to make up the numbers."

Warren has an underlying theme of truthfulness in his personal and business lives that he describes as one of the key character traits to aspire to. As he says, "You don't want to be in business with people who need a contract to be motivated to perform." In the world of business, a manager who is as honest as the day is long is money that is already in the bank.

CHAPTER 10

Manage Costs

"The really good business manager doesn't wake up in the morning and say, 'This is the day that I am going to cut costs,' any more than he wakes up and decides to practice breathing."

—WARREN BUFFETT

Profit is the lifeblood of a business. Lack of profit is the death of a business. The only way to make a profit in business is to have lower costs than the prices you are charging for the products that you sell. The difference between the two is called a profit margin. There is no other way to make money, no other equation. You either make a profit or you don't, and if you don't make a profit, you won't stay in business very long. If you make a lot of profit, you can do more than just make a living—you can become rich.

As managers of a business, we have two main goals: Inspire our sales force to sell as much of the product as possible at the highest possible price, AND inspire our manufacturing and buying teams to produce or acquire the products we sell at the lowest possible prices. It takes two to tango and it takes two to make a profit. The task of keeping costs low is the most important—because it determines the pricing of the product. Lower costs mean that we can sell the product at a lower price, which will make the product more desirable and easier to sell.

The way to determine whether your managers are going to be "cost conscious" is to look at how they handle the seemingly little costs. Warren says, "If managers aren't disciplined on the little things, they will probably be undisciplined on the large things as well." He likes to tell the story of Benjamin Rosner, the owner of Associated Cotton Shops, who was so fanatical about keeping costs low that he once counted the sheets on a roll of toilet paper to make sure that his vendor wasn't cheating him.

Warren also likes to tell about Tom Murphy, CEO of Capital Cities Communications, who was so cost conscious that when he had his office building painted he didn't paint the back wall, because no one could see it. Tom considered public relations and legal departments to be frivolous expenses. He figured that if and when these services were needed, freelancers could be hired at a fraction of the cost. And when he merged Capital Cities with the ABC television network, the first thing he got rid of was ABC's private dining room. Warren loved Tom.

Another aspect of the cost-cutting equation deals with personal savings. If we are in a 40 percent tax bracket, we have to earn $10 to have $6 to spend. So if we reduce our living costs by $6, it is actually the same as making $10 and getting to save $6 of it, which can then be invested. As Benjamin Franklin said, "If you know how to spend less than you get, you have the philosopher's stone." The philosopher's stone was a tool alchemists used to turn lead into gold. In the early part of Warren's life he was fanatical about keeping his living costs low, which is why he drove an old VW Beetle long after he became a multimillionaire. The money he had saved driving a cheap car gave him more money to invest, to make himself even richer.

The bottom line here is this: When Warren looks for a manager, he wants someone who is "cost conscious" as a way of life, not just when the business is starting to fail. Cutting costs is the fastest and easiest way to increase the bottom line of both our businesses and our personal fortunes. Which means that it is the easiest way to get rich (and easy is always a good thing when it comes to making money).

CHAPTER 11

Have an Eye for the Long Term

"There's really a lot of overlap between managing and investing. Being a manager has made me a better investor, and being an investor has made me a better manager."

—WARREN BUFFETT

Warren is a long-term investor. His favorite holding period for companies with exceptional economics working in their favor is forever. This long-term perspective is the fountain that produced his great wealth. But most managers of businesses tend to have a time horizon of under a year. They live in a world defined by quarterly and yearly results. If they surpass quarterly or yearly projections, they'll get fat bonuses and promotions. Fail to bring in quarterly or yearly projections and heads start to roll. This tends to keep management focused on the short term.

This short-term focus almost kills any long-term planning on the part of management. Managers are driven to make the short-term numbers at the cost of long-term planning; they often have no plans to exploit future opportunities, nor do they plan ahead for a potential recession. This is reactive management as opposed to the proactive management that Warren practices. Warren learned from investing that the long-term perspective that had served him so well personally would also serve him well in businesses. One of the first things that Warren asks his managers to do when they join his firm is to stop worrying about the short-term ups and downs of the business and focus on making the business strong and viable for the long term.

Another lesson that Warren learned is that any management's intense focus on the short term tends to make those managers poor allocators of capital. Which creates two very big problems. The first is that management may keep throwing good money after a mediocre business long after it is time to put that capital to use elsewhere. The second is that when management tries to allocate capital outside its core business, it almost always ends up buying a shortsighted promise of prosperity at an inflated price. Warren often cites Coca-Cola's failed venture into the movie business as a perfect example of a great business throwing money after a bad one.

When Warren bought into Berkshire Hathaway, it was a mediocre business that was spending more money than it was earning in a desperate attempt to compete with foreign textile manufacturers. After Warren acquired control, he had the insight to see that it was a dying business, so he stopped spending Berkshire's working capital on the textile business and used it to acquire an insurance company, which is a better business from a long-term perspective. How did he know that the textile business wasn't going to make it and that insurance was going to be a better business? Warren had spent a great amount of time studying a large number of businesses and knew what a great long-term business looked like. This is also how he knew that the textile company was a lousy business, and that no matter how much money he threw at it, its underlying economics would never improve. Eventually Berkshire had to close its textile operations, but by then, its insurance operations were well on their way to helping Berkshire blossom into the financial powerhouse that it is today.

The managers who ran Berkshire's textile operations would have spent the company's last dime trying to stay competitive with foreign manufacturers. It was lucky for Berkshire's sharcholders that Warren had the clarity of vision to see what the future of the textile business looked like, and the foresight to invest the company's working capital in a company that had far better long-term prospects.

Ultimately, Warren learned, when he looks for a great manager, he is also looking for a great investor, whose responsibility is to invest the firm's money in people, products, and new businesses—always with a long-term perspective in mind.

CHAPTER 12

How to Determine Salaries

"If you have a great manager, you want to pay them very well."

—WARREN BUFFETT

Great managers are like great football coaches—they are few and far between. How do you measure whether or not a manager is great? Not all businesses are the same; some businesses have mediocre economics, while others have exceptional economics. Those with exceptional economics working in their favor are often the types of business that make even a lousy manager look good. On the other side, even an exceptional manager may not look too spectacular if he or she is managing a mediocre business. How do we tell the difference? Warren examines how well a manager is doing by measuring the manager's performance against others in his industry.

For example, if we own a business that is earning 20 percent on shareholders' equity, we might think that is great and

53

hand our manager a big bonus check at the end of the year. However, in truth, we may not be doing as well as other businesses in our industry. Do we pay our manager a bonus for giving us a mediocre result compared to others in our own industry? For Warren the answer is no: Unexceptional performance with an exceptional business does not inspire him to dole out exceptional bonuses at the end of the year.

The opposite is true of a business with mediocre economics. If our business is earning 5 percent on equity, we might correctly conclude that, compared to all other businesses, it is on the low end. But comparing it to other businesses within our own industry, we might find that it is on the high end, which would indicate that our manager is keeping us ahead of the pack, and for that, he should be handsomely rewarded.

Warren is a big believer in performance-based pay, as long as it is based on the value added by the manager and not the inherent economics of the business. In Warren's world bonuses are paid according to how much the manager truly improves the underlying economics of the business, not how much the underlying economics enhances the perceived performance of the manager.

MOTIVATE YOUR WORKFORCE

Warren realized early on that if he was to delegate to the point of abdication, motivating his managers to achieve exceptional levels of performance would be his primary function. Once he found the right businesses and put the right managers in place, all he had left to do was motivate his managers to be all that they can be.

In this portion of the book we present the management motivational skills that Warren uses. We explain what he learned from Carnegie and others and how he adapted this into a winning management style. From first impression, to using praise, to understanding the dangers of using criticism, to the subtle use of suggestion, Warren is masterful in inspiring and influencing his managers. We begin by examining his use of first impression to set the stage.

CHAPTER 13

Make a Good First Impression

When you meet someone for the first time, begin the encounter in a friendly way.

Beryl Raff was a successful Dallas jewelry executive heading up J. C. Penney's retail jewelry division. Then in the spring of 2009 she got a call from a friend in the business asking her if she would be interested in interviewing for the job of CEO of Berkshire's Helzberg Diamond Shops. Helzberg's is a ninety-year-old chain of 240 jewelry stores and the life's work of "Diamond King" Barnett Helzberg before he sold out to Berkshire.

Beryl had long admired Warren and his company, Berkshire Hathaway. She knew the quality of the people who worked for him, the multitude of great businesses that he owned, and his stellar reputation as an enlightened CEO. She knew that his managers sang him praise after praise, and thought the opportunity of working for such a first-rate outfit might be the chance of a lifetime. Merely talking to Warren would be a highlight of her career. What she did not expect was to see Warren picking her up at the airport himself, in his gold Cadillac. As nervous as Beryl was, Warren immediately put her at ease. She found him witty and charming. After spending a couple of hours at his office answering questions about her vision for the jewelry business, Warren took her to a delightful lunch at his country club, gave her a tour of his hometown, and then offered her the job. She thought it over for a couple of days and then accepted and has been happy ever since. Beryl says that even after just a few months on the job, she already feels like an adopted member of Warren's extended family.

Warren recognizes the importance of making first encounters friendly. He started his meeting with Beryl by meeting her and offering her a ride. He was light, funny, friendly, and eager to put her at ease. He took her to lunch and listened to her. Her first impression? *This is a guy I would love to work for,* and Warren continues to make her feel like a special member of the Berkshire Hathaway family. She has said that her greatest fear is disappointing him.

Imagine if Warren had done just the opposite. What if he hadn't picked Beryl up at the airport? What if he had made her take a cab instead? Imagine he didn't even take her to lunch or listen to her. Her first impression might have been that Warren was a distant billionaire who only cared about whether or not she could make him more money, the kind of boss she wouldn't like working for. If that had been the case, she probably wouldn't have taken the job.

The rule is simple: If you want to get your way, start your encounters with other people in a friendly way. As Warren has discovered, it's the only way that pays.

CHAPTER 14

The Power of Praise

We all have a deep and honest need to be appreciated.

Warren recognizes that we all have a need to feel important. It is almost biological. Early American psychologist and philosopher William James once said, "The deepest principle in human nature is the need to be appreciated." This is not lost on Warren.

One of the great early managers whom Warren studied was Charles Schwab, the former head of the United States Steel Company. Schwab was the first superstar manager and the first CEO to be paid a million dollars a year. What made Schwab the most revered manager of his day was not his knowledge of the steel industry, which even he admitted wasn't extensive, but rather his ability to inspire enthusiasm in his employees. He did that through appreciation and encouragement.

Schwab said, "I consider my ability to arouse enthusiasm

to be my greatest asset, and the way to develop the best that is in a person is by appreciation and encouragement. There is nothing that kills the ambitions of a person as much as criticisms from superiors. I never criticize anyone. I believe in giving people incentive to work. So I am anxious to praise but loath to find fault. If I like anything, I am hearty in my appreciation and hearty in my praise."

Schwab noted that his boss Andrew Carnegie had even gone so far as to praise his employees publicly as well as privately. Warren follows Schwab's advice as if it were creed, praising employees and managers for the small things and gushing over them for the big. He is the consummate cheerleader and his employees' biggest fan. He never misses a chance to praise his managers in private or at Berkshire's annual meetings and in its annual reports. Warren learned from Schwab that if he praised people for the little things, they'd give him even bigger things to praise them for later on down the line.

For Warren, praise truly is the gift that keeps on giving.

CHAPTER 15

The Power Reputation

Give your employees a fine reputation to live up to and praise them every chance you get.

W arren learned the importance of giving your employees a fine reputation to live up to from Carnegie, who stressed the point to his readers by telling the following story.

A manager worked with a long-time trusted older employee, who had become bored and lackadaisical about his work, resulting in a lowering of the worker's craftsmanship and productivity. The manager reviewed his options. He could fire the older employee, but then he would have to replace him. He could threaten him with being fired, but the worker would probably resent him. Instead he chose to talk to the employee one on one, friend to friend. In the course of the conversation, he told the worker that he was one of his best employees, that he was an inspiration to other employees, and that many customers in the past had complimented his craftsmanship. But as of late, he said, the employee's work had slipped. The manager said he was worried about him and was wondering if there was anything he could do to help. How did the worker respond? Realizing he had a fine reputation to live up to, he stopped doing shoddy work, increased the level of his production, and returned to being the worker that other workers looked up to.

Warren praises his managers as being the best in the business. He notes this admiration in his annual letters to Berkshire's shareholders, mentions it at Berkshire's annual meeting, and talks about it when interviewed by the press. He never misses an opportunity to give his managers a fine reputation to live up to, which is easy for him to do since they are the best in the business.

ADVICE TO BONO

Warren's theory on giving his managers a fine reputation to live up to dovetails with the advice he gave the rock star Bono, who sought out Warren's advice on how to inspire Americans to help him in his battle against poverty in Africa. Warren told him: "Don't appeal to the conscience of America. Appeal to the greatness of America and you'll get the job done."

Appealing to a person's conscience means subtly appealing to his or her sense of right or wrong. What kind of person are you if you don't want to help poor, starving people in Africa? This plays on our sense of guilt. We tend not to like people who make us feel guilty; in fact we spend most of our time trying to avoid them.

Instead Warren advised Bono to speak to the American people's sense of greatness. Imagine how a statement like this—that plays to people's sense of guilt—would've made Bono's American listeners feel: "All these poor people are starving in Africa; are you, the richest nation on earth, just going to sit there and let them starve?" Now compare it to: "You're the most intelligent nation on earth, you won World War II against impossible odds, and you pierced the heavens to put a man on the moon. When I was confronted with this tremendous problem of helping the poor, suffering, lost souls in Africa, I thought, to whom should I turn? Then I had an epiphany; I should turn to the greatest nation in the world, the one people that can solve really tough problems, the one nation that can accomplish the impossible." Warren advised Bono to appeal to America's sense of pride, its sense of greatness, its fine reputation. Give a person or a nation a fine reputation to live up to and they *will* live up to it. Make them feel guilty and ashamed and they will disappoint you.

Using guilt is not productive. Appealing to the greatness of others is what works for Warren, and it will work for you. Most important, it works for the employees and managers you are trying to inspire.

CHAPTER 16

The Dangers of Criticism

Using criticism to motivate is futile because it puts a person on the defensive, wounds his precious pride, hurts his sense of importance, and arouses resentment.

Warren has discovered that uninvited criticism is something we all hate to hear. It breeds resentment. It can drive us out of our parents' house as young adults. It has been the cause of many a failed marriage. Yet many of us make the mistake of bestowing uninvited criticism on others, especially in the workplace. Warren learned long ago that criticism was not the way to inspire his managers; it doesn't make for lasting change, and it destroys any kind of productive working relationship.

Instead of criticizing his managers when they make mistakes, Warren tries to understand what went wrong and why there was an error in judgment. He pays attention to his managers and their work environments, and he imagines himself in their shoes. And as long as his managers are taking intelligent risks, he affords them the luxury of making the occasional mistake.

Let's take a look at Warren in action:

David Sokol is one of Warren's top managers; he runs Berkshire's MidAmerican Energy Company. David once spent $360 million on a zinc project that failed and had to be written off as a loss. David fully expected Warren to fire him for his colossal error in judgment. Instead of firing him or berating him with criticism, Warren, upon hearing the bad news, simply told David, "We all make mistakes." Warren went on to say that he had made even bigger mistakes during his tenure at the helm of Berkshire Hathaway and told David to learn from his error, but not to dwell on it.

David thinks the world of Warren and has never made a similar mistake. On the contrary, for the last nine years he has done a brilliant job leading Berkshire's energy operations to become some of the most profitable in the industry.

But had Warren berated him, mocked his stupidity and foolishness, and criticized him, David would have come to despise Warren, and it is doubtful that he would have been inspired to stay on and build Warren's MidAmerican Energy into the money-making powerhouse that it is today.

Warren knows that praise and criticism are two of the most important tools a manager has at his or her disposal. Used correctly, these tools can inspire employees to work hard, be creative, and achieve great success. Used incorrectly, they can destroy drive, ambition, and creativity, and almost certainly ensure failure. Warren feels that learning how to effectively use praise and criticism is the primary motivational task of a manager. A manager who fully understands this challenge has the ability to motivate others to greatness regardless of the task, be that motivating a production team to be more efficient and effective or getting his own children to do their homework.

Warren is a genius at using both praise and criticism. His rule is simple: Praise by name and criticize by category. Let's take a look at what he means.

We all crave praise. Nothing makes us feel better about ourselves or inspires us more to do better, beginning in early childhood when we vie to win the praise of our parents, later on seek it from our teachers, and in the workplace look for it from our boss. We need praise; it tells us that we are on the right path, and it inspires us to stay on that path and to do even better.

No one likes criticism. Nothing can make us feel more terrible about ourselves than to be criticized for something we did or didn't do. Nothing will inspire us less. We hated to hear criticism as children and we hate to hear it as adults. Criticism means that we got it wrong, that this isn't the right path for us, that we should stop what we are doing and try again, or give up and do something else. We often dislike people who criticize us, which means that we won't listen to them; we shut them out.

Nothing will win you friends faster than praise, and nothing will make you enemies faster than criticism.

Many managers never learn how praise and criticism interact. This is one of Warren's greatest management secrets—using both praise and criticism to inspire a person to achieve more.

Warren sets the stage with praise, praising both the small accomplishments and the big achievements. He never misses an opportunity to praise his managers, and he is a master at remembering names and praising people by name. Why? Because nothing is sweeter to another person than the sound of his or her own name. Read an annual report written by Warren Buffett and you will see that it is loaded with praise for his managers, who are singled out by name. He is generous in spreading praise around.

Warren elevates his managers to a lofty position and makes them feel special by continuing to praise them in person and in print. Work becomes more than just a place to make a buck; it becomes a place to boost self-esteem.

Once Warren's managers respect and trust him and

believe that he has their best interests at heart, he is in a much better position to offer them advice. Here he employs a bit of "magic" as well: He never criticizes the manager directly. When a manager with whom Warren has built a solid relationship asks his opinion of a business idea, and Warren is not keen on it, he will make a subtle suggestion, leaving the manager to draw his or her own conclusion. A classic Warren response would be to acknowledge the manager's idea, to say that it is enticing, and then to offer a story where he, Warren, or another businessman had a similar idea that led to disaster, thereby leaving the manager to draw his own conclusion.

Warren applies the same theory when talking about the world at large—he is quick to praise an individual banker for his or her integrity, but if he is unhappy with the banker, he will only criticize the banking profession as a whole. The banker saves face and Warren gets his point across without making an enemy.

As Warren says, "Praise the person, criticize the category."

If You Must Criticize Someone Personally, Praise Them First

Although Warren realizes that personal criticism is poisonous, he is also a realist. He recognizes that in some cases criticism is unavoidable. When personal criticism is necessary, he follows the advice of Carnegie, who suggested that one should compliment the person first. Criticism by itself is almost always flat out rejected. However, when criticism is preceded by praise, the listener is more accepting of the suggestion.

Someone bestowing a compliment is perceived as a friend, someone we like. The people we like are those whose opinions matter to us. A compliment creates the trust that is necessary for constructive criticism to be heard and acted upon.

Warren used the praise/criticism model to pacify Berkshire shareholders who were angry with him for investing in PetroChina—because PetroChina's parent company, China National Petroleum Corporation (CNPC), was making investments in Sudan. After the shareholders had made their protests, Warren began by praising their social consciousness and appreciation of the seriousness of the situation in the Sudan. Then and only then did he offer criticism of their position, arguing that since PetroChina was a subsidiary of the CNPC, Berkshire had no way to influence it.

Here are some general examples of the praise/criticism model: 1) Business: "Johnny, you are doing a wonderful job handling the daily mail. You're a great improvement over the last guy we had in this job. I'm very happy with your performance. However, your approach to handling customer complaints is still a little rough. May I offer you a few suggestions?"

2) Family: "I can see by your report card that you are doing very well in spelling, which is fantastic. I'm very proud of you for doing so well. However, you seem to be running into some difficulties in math. I had that problem when I was your age, and I was wondering if you might be open to me lending a hand in getting you over this rough spot?"

The rule here is pretty straightforward: Avoid using criticism as if it were the plague, but when you have to, praise the person first and then criticize the category. If that doesn't work, praise the person first before you criticize him directly. This approach works for Warren and it will work for anyone who is willing to open the door first with sweet praises.

CHAPTER 17

How to Win an Argument

To win an argument, you sometimes have to lose.

Warren learned early on that the way to win an argument was not to have one in the first place; that to openly correct someone might cause them to lose face, and in the process the person could end up resenting them. Warren learned from Carnegie that instead of taking issue with someone, it was better to agree with them so that you could win the person's trust, and in the process, get the person to listen to your ideas. Warren fully embraces this philosophy, and he is famous for avoiding conflict and arguments.

Warren is also well known for listening to people and for respecting their opinions, even when they are contrary to his own. But it is his ability to agree with the other person's argument that allows others to relax and to hear Warren's position. And Warren knows that getting the other person to listen to you is the first step to winning any argument.

An example: If young Warren, as a securities salesman, was out selling GEICO stock and went to visit a potential client who told him that he preferred to invest in Philip Morris, Warren, instead of arguing with him, would agree that Philip Morris was a great company and a wise investment. This would put an immediate end to potential conflict and allow Warren to then engage the client in a discussion about the wonderful virtues of GEICO.

THE INFLUENCE OF BENJAMIN FRANKLIN

The wisdom of American Founding Father Benjamin Franklin has played an important role in the education of both Warren and his partner Charlie Munger. At Berkshire shareholder meetings and in annual reports, they are both quick to cite Franklin's influence on their business and life philosophies. Thus, it is no surprise that Franklin's strategy of avoiding arguments and respecting other people's opinions found its way into Warren's quiver of ways to get people to listen to his ideas. We've picked a small piece from Franklin's autobiography that Warren found influential on this point.

Here is what Franklin had to say:

I made it a rule to forbear all direct contradictions to the sentiments of others, and all positive assertion of my own.

I even forbade myself the use of every word or expression in the language that imported a fixed opinion, such as "certainly," "undoubtedly," etc. I adopted instead of them "I conceive," "I apprehend," or "I imagine" a thing to be so or so; or, "so it appears to me at present." When another asserted something that I thought an error, I denied myself the pleasure of contradicting him abruptly, and of showing him immediately some absurdity in his proposition. In answering I began by observing that in certain cases or circumstances his opinion would be right, but in the present case there appeared or seemed to me some difference, etc. I soon found the advantage of this change in my manner; the conversations I engaged in went on more pleasantly. The modest way in which I proposed my opinions procured them a readier reception and less contradiction. I had less mortification when I was found to be in the wrong, and I more easily prevailed with others to give up their mistakes and join with me when I happened to be in the right.

Franklin explained that his ability to persuade his fellow countrymen to follow his ideas was a result of this approach. Warren has learned that avoiding arguments and accepting others' opinions is one of the secrets to getting other people to listen to you. Which just happens to be a very helpful skill to have if you are trying to build fantastic fortunes and great nations.

CHAPTER 18

Speak to the Other Person's
Wants and Needs

When you want someone to do something, stop thinking in terms of what you want and think in terms of what they want.

Warren has learned that discovering what his managers need or want and being able to speak to their needs and wants is one of the great secrets to being successful as a manager and as a business owner.

One of Warren's early influences in this area was Henry Ford, the great industrialist of the twentieth century. Ford, in his autobiography, said, "If there is any one secret of success, it lies in the ability to get the other person's point of view and see things from that person's angle as well as from our own."

Warren incorporated this idea into both his family and business lives. When he wanted his children to do something or to change their behavior, instead of nagging or criticizing them, he spoke to their wants. If he wanted them to lose weight, he offered a reward for weight loss, which spoke to their teenage want of ready cash.

When seeking to buy a privately held family business for Berkshire Hathaway, Warren speaks to the owner's pride in the business. He understands that the owner may want to sell the company for the most money possible, but that person also needs to make sure that the company's loyal employees are well taken care of and that once sold, the company isn't broken apart and sold off piece by piece. Over the years, Warren has enticed more than a dozen businessmen and women to sell their privately held companies to him even when those owners had been offered more money by other companies and leveraged buyout firms. In the case of the Nebraska Furniture Mart, owner Rose Blumkin had been offered eighty million dollars for the entire company by a German conglomerate. She wanted the money, but really didn't want to give up running the business she had built and loved. So instead of selling out to the Germans, she sold 90 percent of it to Warren for forty million dollars, because he agreed that Mrs. B and her sons could stay on and continue running the entire show. Warren got a fantastic business at a great price, with the brilliant Mrs. B and her all-star management team thrown in to the deal, all because he spoke to her needs.

And there is little doubt that A. L. Ueltschi, founder and chairman of FlightSafety, would have gotten more money if he had sold out to a leverage buyout firm, but Warren spoke to his needs and offered him the best of both worlds: a ton of money and the chance to keep working at what he loves to do—which is running FlightSafety. What did Warren get? He got a terrific business—run by a genius of a man—at a price that still keeps him smiling.

Does it get any better than that?

CHAPTER 19

Encourage Others to Come Up
with the Right Idea

*Inducing the other person to come up with the right idea
is far more powerful as a motivational tool than telling
them the right idea.*

Warren is famous for hiring people and then not telling
them what to do. Instead he lets them set their own goals
and standards. Invariably, they set the bar higher than he
would have. Warren's managers would say that even though
he never tells them what he expects from them, they know
that he expects a great deal. His silence induces his managers
to imagine that he expects a lot, and this becomes the reality
that drives their performance.

Tell someone to do something and it becomes an order.
No one likes to be ordered about. We naturally resist anyone
who gives us orders. However, if it is "our idea," we treat it

as gospel and act on it with purpose and conviction. We are in control.

A perfect example is a motivational story that Carnegie used to tell about an auto dealership sales manager who, after many failed attempts at motivating his salesmen, finally called his sales team together and asked them to tell him what they expected of him as a manager. As he listened to their answers, he wrote them out on a blackboard. Then he asked what he had a right to expect from them. They spoke right up, saying that he could expect them to be honest, hard-working team players, and that they would show initiative and optimism. They set their own standards. Did they live up to them? Not only did they live up to them, they far exceeded them, bringing in record sales.

It's a very simple concept that is easy to put into action in our everyday lives.

Here are a few examples:

Instead of ordering someone not to do something, illustrate the negative consequences of doing it. "Don't swim in the lake" becomes "There are crocodiles in the lake and they like to eat little children." The child is then induced into thinking of the crocodiles eating him, which compels him not to swim in the lake.

Instead of ordering someone to do something, illustrate the positive consequences of doing it. "I want sales production to increase" becomes "If sales production increases, it will make me happy and I'll be able to pay bigger bonuses at Christmas." The workers realize that an increase in sales will make for a happy manager and bigger Christmas bonuses.

If you are wondering how to better manage your children, try using the same method. Sit your children down at the beginning of the school year and ask them what they expect out of you in the coming year. List their expectations, discussing them as you go. When you are finished, and are comfortable with their expectations, agree to them. Then ask what you can expect out of them. You just might be shocked at how demanding they can be of themselves.

Ask Questions Instead of Giving Direct Orders

As we just said, Warren is famous among his managers for never giving a direct order. He is also well known for asking tons of questions.

Warren recognizes that no one likes to get a direct order, just as no one likes being told what to do. Bossy managers are usually hated and are the least likely to inspire workers to excel. A direct order might work in the military, but in civilian life it can cause lingering bitterness that drags on performance.

Warren learned that great managers give their orders indirectly by way of making suggestions. One way to make suggestions is simply by asking questions. Asking questions makes your suggestion more palatable and often stimulates employees to come up with their own ideas for solving the problem. We are more willing to act on our own ideas than to act on another's ideas, especially when we are being ordered around. It is always better to let people figure something out for themselves. If that is not possible, then give them a little nudge in the right direction with a suggestion framed as a question.

Here are a few examples of how to use a question to convert a direct order, which will offend employees, into a suggestion, which will stimulate them to willingly act:

Direct order: "I want that job done by Monday."

Suggestion: "It would be great if we could get that job done by Monday; do you think you can come up with a way to do that?"

Direct order: "Slow down, you are driving too fast!"

Suggestion: "You know the roads are rather slick; do you think that if we slowed down that that would make it safer?"

Direct order: "That is not the way to do it."

Suggestion: "Can you think of a better way to do that?"

Direct order: "I want you to do it this way."

Suggestion: "Do you think that if we did it this way that it would turn out better?"

Direct order: "When we go to the zoo, I want you to stay by my side."

Suggestion: "When we go to the zoo, can you think of any reasons why you should stay by my side?"

Warren seldom gives a direct order, but he is famous for peppering his managers with lots of questions. Now you know why.

CHAPTER 20

Everyone Makes Mistakes—Admit It!

When we are wrong, we should admit it quickly and emphatically.

W arren believes that when people are wrong, they should be right up-front about it, and admit it quickly and emphatically. To do otherwise would give the impression that we are trying to hide something, or that we have neither the courage nor the integrity to admit when we are wrong. This kind of behavior leads people to mistrust us. No one can stand anyone who is always right, and no one can stand someone who won't admit when they are wrong. And if they won't admit when they are wrong, what else are they lying about? The accounting books, maybe?

Also, managers who don't or refuse to admit that they are wrong cause a kind of festering distrust among their employees. They become less respectful, less willing to follow, more distrustful of management's recommendations and guidance.

Warren is always up-front about any and all mistakes that he makes, is forthcoming with his managers when he blows it, and is the first to admit to shareholders when he screws up. And they love him for it. When he recently made a bad investment in a couple of Irish banks that cost Berkshire several hundred million, he was right up-front about it. When he blew an investment in ConocoPhillips, an oil company he had bought into when oil was $140 a barrel, his error cost Berkshire $2 billion, but he didn't hesitate for a second to admit to Berkshire's shareholders his mistake. He didn't try to blame someone else, or say that other people had made similar mistakes, he just said that he made an error in judgment and it was his fault.

By admitting when he is wrong, and being forthcoming about it, Warren wins the trust of his employees and shareholders alike, and at the same time avoids all the political fallout that has taken down great men since the beginning of time.

MANAGERIAL PITFALLS, CHALLENGES, AND LEARNING OPPORTUNITIES

The final chapters in this book include some of Warren's important axioms regarding the dangers of borrowing too much money, employees breaking the law, good ideas gone astray, making mistakes, managing sycophants, missing opportunities, seeing the road ahead, and a few bits of wisdom for managing our own lives. All learned the hard way, by experience. Weigh them carefully, as they will not only help keep you out of managerial trouble, they will also help get you out of it.

CHAPTER 21

The Hidden Dangers of Making
a Living on Borrowed Money

*"The roads of business are riddled with potholes; a plan
that requires dodging them all is a plan for disaster."*

—WARREN BUFFETT

Managers of businesses that have to borrow a lot of
money are gambling that they won't hit any economic potholes in the road ahead. Their business plan requires dodging problems. But even the best-run businesses can't dodge
problems forever, if they're heavily leveraged, which is why
every twenty years or so we have a banking crisis. Banks are
the kings of leverage; they have to borrow all that money they
lend out, and most of that money was borrowed short term
and loaned out long term. When those people who loaned
money to the bank short term want it back, and the bank
can't pay it back, well, that is when things start to get messy.

Economic change can offer lots of opportunity, provided that we have the cash to take advantage of it. Economic change can also mean disaster if we have taken on too much debt to survive it. Life is full of economic change—always has been, always will be.

"Leverage is very tempting and always leads to trouble."

—WARREN BUFFETT

The temptation of leverage is that it can dramatically improve the performance of any business for the manager who learns how to use it. Let's say that in a normal year the business you manage earns a $6 million profit without any debt. You have a business opportunity that costs $100 million but will earn $15 million a year. This sounds promising, doesn't it? The catch is that your business doesn't have the $100 million needed to finance the deal. Your friendly Wall Street bank is more than willing to loan you the $100 million if you agree to pay it $10 million a year in interest. This means that after paying the $10 million in interest, you will earn a net profit of $5 million on the $15 million in new business. Add in the $6 million on the old business, and your company is now earning a total of $11 million. Make the deal and you almost double your net earnings. Guess who gets the big bonus at the end of the year? You do, for your brilliant managing of the company's assets.

With the Wall Street investment banks, the game of leverage was played out to an extreme. Borrow $100 billion at 5 percent short term and loan it out at 7 percent long term, and suddenly your firm is earning $2 billion a year in profit and the financial press is writing about your $50 million salary.

Now you know why managers tend to push their companies to take on as much leverage/debt as they can possibly put to profitable use.

However, there is a catch, and it is a big one. What happens if there is a recession and your company's business income makes a dramatic drop, to the point that you cannot generate enough money to service the debt? In this case, you would start burning up the company's net worth until either the economy turned around and business improved, or you were forced to put the company into bankruptcy. When companies begin contemplating bankruptcy, the company's old management is usually the first to go.

However, if the company hadn't taken on the $100 million debt, when the recession hits, all the company would have to do is cut back production to the point that it would meet the new lower level of demand, at which point it would start making money again. Yes, people would have lost their jobs, but the survival of the company would not be in question.

When Warren looked at a company during the '50s and '60s, he always asked how did it manage through the Great Depression? Did it do well? Or did it fail? This told him a great deal about the historical nature of the company and its need to use debt. Warren still looks at the long-term historic performance of a company; he often mentions that companies that he has major investments in, like Coca-Cola and Wells Fargo, have hundred-year histories. These are businesses that not only survived the Great Depression, they are companies that are going to survive the current recession as well. But he still keeps a watchful eye on how much debt all the companies he owns carry, knowing that in hard times it can kill even the best of businesses.

Warren's own Berkshire Hathaway has long avoided going into debt; if Warren can't pay for it with cash, he isn't interested. Warren even takes it further by letting cash pile up if he can't find a good value, which also protects Berkshire against hard times. In the heat of the Great Recession of '09, Berkshire was sitting on very little debt and only a very comfortable cushion of twenty billion dollars in cash. This gave Warren plenty of restful nights and the economic firepower to take advantage of the lower stock prices that the recession brought.

Old-school managers like Warren are very reluctant to use debt to improve earnings. They lived through the hard times and have the scars to prove it. But in the last fifteen years, the quick buck meant fast promotions and big bonuses, so the new generation piled on the debt, and in the Great

Recession of '09, many found themselves dangling over the abyss of financial failure and the sudden end of their briefly successful careers.

Sometimes old dogs know all the tricks.

CHAPTER 22

Do Good Ideas Always Bear Fruit?

"You can get into way more trouble with a good idea than a bad idea."

—WARREN BUFFETT

This is Warren quoting his late mentor, Benjamin Graham, who taught Warren to take heed of the potential danger of a good idea. Managers never act on ideas they know are bad; these are killed at the start. But a good idea is acted upon, and if it is successful it becomes an institution. Subprime mortgages were originally a good idea; they allowed good people with marginal credit to buy homes, and mortgage brokers to make money. But eventually people with poor credit histories were qualifying for subprime mortgages. More people got homes and more mortgage brokers got even more money. Then one day we woke up to a recession and people started losing their jobs, and they didn't have the money to make their subprime mortgage payments. Suddenly the great idea started to turn into a disaster.

The same thing occurred with the insurance giant AIG, which sold insurance to banks and other institutions to cover the risk of default on a large number of investment-grade corporate bonds. AIG figured that the risk that thousands of corporations all over the world would go bust at the same time was practically zero and that the premiums that banks and institutions paid would never have to be paid out in claims. AIG raked it in, earning hundreds of millions in premiums. It was low-risk, easy money.

Then one day the banks showed up wanting AIG to insure several groups of subprime loans that had been packaged together like the corporate bonds had been. AIG figured that since writing insurance on the corporate bonds was making them a ton of money, writing insurance on a pool of subprime mortgages would also be profitable. But they didn't bother to sit down and really figure out the risk of a large pool of subprime mortgages going belly up. And then the recession hit and hundreds of thousands of subprime mortgages started going into default, and prices on the subprime bonds that AIG had insured started falling, and as they dropped, AIG had to put up more and more collateral to support its subprime insurance contracts. Then things went from bad to worse, and AIG ran out of assets it could put up as additional collateral; suddenly the company was at risk of defaulting on all of its subprime insurance contracts that it had sold to the financial institutions of the world.

If AIG defaulted, all those banks and institutions it sold contracts to would be left with uninsured bond portfolios. This means the banks and institutions would be stuck for every dollar of decline in value that their bond portfolios suffered—a little like not having insurance on your house when it burns down. The prospect of AIG failing to post more collateral essentially threatened to render a great many of the world's financial institutions insolvent, which would have meant a complete collapse of the world economy. Which is why the U.S. Treasury stepped in with an $85 billion loan to AIG—because the entire game was on the table.

In the end a really great idea—insuring investment-grade corporate debt—got AIG into insuring pools of subprime mortgages, which turned out to be a really, really bad idea for AIG and the rest of the world.

As Warren says, you can get into a lot more trouble with a good idea than a bad one.

CHAPTER 23

How to Handle Employees
Who Break the Law

"There is plenty of money to be made in the center of the court. There is no need to play around the edges."

—WARREN BUFFETT

This is the advice that Warren gave the managers of his companies after the fallout of the Salomon Brothers bond-trading scandal. Salomon Brothers was a Wall Street investment bank famous for its bond-trading prowess. In the late 1980s, Warren invested $700 million in the company's preferred stock. In 1991, two Salomon bond traders broke the U.S. Treasury's bidding rules for buying Treasury Bonds. They were caught submitting false bids to the U.S. Treasury in an attempt to take a larger share of the new issue of Treasury Bonds than the U.S. Treasury permitted. Salomon's management, upon discovering the illegal acts of its traders, was not forthcoming to the Securities and Exchange Commission or to the U.S. Treasury.

This led Treasury to consider barring Salomon from trading in Treasuries, which would have been a certain deathblow to the company and to Warren's investment. At the request of Salomon's board of directors, Warren stepped in as chairman of the board and immediately cleaned house at Salomon, removing its CEO and the top managers who had been involved in supervising the traders who made the false bids. He also instigated an up-front policy with the U.S. Treasury, giving investigators free access to Salomon's records. In the end Salomon had to pay a hefty $290 million fine, but it got to keep trading in Treasuries, which meant that it got to stay in business.

Warren conveyed this lesson to his managers: While it is important to be aggressive in making money, you can make the money you need by staying within the boundaries of the law. When managers break the law in the name of making a quick buck, they risk losing their entire business with one single action. In Salomon's case, the bond trader bet the entire company for a slightly larger piece of the U.S. government bond market.

As managers, we have to keep a watchful eye on our employees to make sure that they don't bet the store in an attempt to further their careers. And when we catch employees doing something illegal, the first call we make is to the authorities. Not to make the call is to become an accessory after the fact, which is also a crime. It's a hard lesson that no one wants to learn firsthand.

CHAPTER 24

Dealing with Your Mistakes

"I make plenty of mistakes and I'll make plenty more mistakes, too. That's part of the game. You've just got to make sure that the right things overcome the wrong ones."

— WARREN BUFFETT

N o one is perfect, and that includes Warren. Mistakes are a part of the landscape and there is no getting away from them. The trick to remember is that our successes in life must outweigh our mistakes. Reverse the equation and we end up in trouble.

Warren's mistakes include paying too much for a business—ConocoPhillips and the then-named USAir; buying into a sinking business—Blue Chip Stamp; and not buying into the right business at the right time—he initially thumbed his nose at Capital Cities Broadcasting. He also made some serious mistakes in the handling of his managers—he hired himself to run his insurance operations (which proved to be a bad idea)—and, to run Dempster Mills, the first manager he hired was a loser, the second one a winner. Yet he still ended up the richest man in the world.

The way in which Warren deals with his mistakes sets him apart from the competition. He learns from mistakes, but he doesn't dwell on them. Those who dwell on their mistakes waste an enormous amount of time and energy that could be spent on developing new ways to make money and enjoy life.

Mistakes are part of the past, and short of remembering their lessons, Warren says that they should stay there, since all the money to be made is somewhere in the future.

CHAPTER 25

Sycophants— Are They an Asset or a Liability?

"Of one thing be certain: If a CEO is enthused about a particularly foolish acquisition, both his internal staff and his outside advisers will come up with whatever projections are needed to justify his stance. Only in fairy tales are emperors told that they are naked."

—WARREN BUFFETT

Leaders love to be loved, and in the process of needing to be loved, they surround themselves with yes people. Yes people make their living telling the boss how wonderful he or she is and how great his or her ideas are, even when that is not true. Why don't they tell the truth? Because that isn't their job. Their job is to say yes to the boss. For that, they are handsomely rewarded.

Every business has sycophants, creeping around the corners, sucking up to the boss and reinventing the truth. Hire an adviser and his job likely becomes to advise you to do what you wanted to do in the first place. Advisers who voice dissent too often are soon out of a job. Most people don't keep "no men" around.

What's wrong with surrounding yourself with yes men? Nothing, until the disaster that could have been foreseen drops into your lap and your board of directors is asking you to resign. Wall Street is littered with the remains of CEOs who let their yes men convince them that their companies could manage the risk of derivatives. When the CEOs figured out that the risk couldn't be managed, it was too late for them and their companies.

Warren's solution is to surround himself with as few people as possible; in fact he often has said that his idea of a group decision is to look in the mirror. He also seeks the counsel of Berkshire's vice chairman, Charlie Munger, who says "no" ten times as often as he says "yes." Warren thinks of Charlie as his "no man," and while Charlie's "no" may never make him the life of the party, it has kept Warren from stepping into disaster on more than one occasion.

CHAPTER 26

Learn from Missed Opportunities

"Since mistakes of omission don't appear in financial statements, most people don't pay attention to them. We rub our noses in mistakes of omission."

— WARREN BUFFETT

Even the best manager misses opportunities, and this often goes completely unnoticed. In the world of investing, and in managing Berkshire, Warren freely admits he missed more opportunities than he should have—he laments not getting in early on Wal-Mart and Walgreens. When Warren does miss an opportunity, he likes to spend a little time contemplating why it didn't cross his radar screen or why he saw it but didn't act. He does this with the hope that his reevaluation of the situation will enlighten him enough that he won't repeat the same mistake in the future.

In Warren's world there are two basic kinds of missed opportunities: (1) ones we missed because they weren't on our horizon; and (2) ones we saw but failed to act on. These are the most frustrating because they were looking us right in the face.

If the opportunity simply wasn't on our horizon, the solution is to expand our field of search. There is a whole world of business brokers and investment bankers that are more than happy to show us potential opportunities.

As for the opportunities that we can see but don't act on, the most common reason for missing one is that we erred in calculating the risk involved. These are opportunities that we would have liked to have acted on, but mistakenly deemed as too risky.

Mistakes of omission due to miscalculation of risk are the easiest to understand: We took in all the information we had available and made a judgment call based on that information. If we don't have the right knowledge, we can't competently make the judgment call. This is why Warren lets the managers of his individual companies make even the biggest decisions regarding the companies they run—he trusts that they know their game better than he does.

But mistakes of omission that occur because we didn't have our eyes open to opportunity are errors that speak to our management ability and organizational skills. A good manager is always looking for opportunity and has put the necessary infrastructure in place to assist him.

The best managers follow Warren's example—they examine the opportunities they missed and ask the hard questions as to why they missed them. Then the next time around they just might catch the brass ring instead of watching it slip through their fingers.

CHAPTER 27

Bank On the Tried and True

"You don't have to think of everything. It was Isaac New-
ton who said, 'I've seen a little more of the world because
I stood on the shoulders of giants.' There is nothing wrong
with standing on other people's shoulders."

—WARREN BUFFETT

One of the great errors of young managers is that they think that they have to have an original idea or some stroke of creative genius to catapult them to the top. These brilliant ideas, more often than not, lead to costly folly.

Warren has discovered that the best ideas in business and life are the ones that are tried and true, where the chance of failure is almost nil. Where do these proven ideas come from? They come from other people and businesses that have successfully put them to work.

By studying successful businesses, we can get dozens of great ideas about how to do something right, and by studying unsuccessful businesses, we learn how easy it is to do something wrong.

Miles Davis, the great jazz musician, once remarked, "Lesser artists borrow, great artists steal." The same can be said of great business managers. If we see a great idea, we should steal it and immediately put it to use. Where do we find these wonderful ideas? By studying the competition to see what they are doing right and what they did that was wrong.

Rose Blumkin, who founded the Nebraska Furniture Mart in the 1930s, brought with her from Russia the simple merchandising concept of discounting prices in the name of increasing volume, which she implemented at her store. The local established merchants refused to discount, and Rose took away tons of their business, so much in fact that they sued her for unfair trade practices. Her defense was simple—the other merchants charged too much. The judge ruled in Rose's favor and the next day he and his wife went down to her store and bought carpeting for their home. Rose didn't invent discounting; she borrowed an idea that merchants were using in Russia and used it to make money in her new home in America.

Jack Ringwalt owned and operated a small insurance company called National Indemnity, in Warren's hometown of Omaha. Jack ran his company with a keen eye on costs, and was fanatical about underwriting discipline; he would only write insurance if he knew it would make him money. If rates dropped he simply stopped writing policies, even if it meant having his staff sit around doing nothing—which he could afford to do because he had built up a surplus of capital during the good times. He once told Warren, "There is no such thing as a bad risk. There are only bad rates." Jack made himself rich running his business this way. And when Warren bought National Indemnity, he not only kept Jack's philosophy of disciplined underwriting in place, he put it into practice in every insurance company that he has invested in since. Disciplined underwriting has allowed Berkshire to grow from being a small insurance company in Omaha to one of the largest insurance operations in the world.

You don't have to stand on top of Mount Everest to know that it's high, and you don't have to be a genius to identify a great manager or a well-run business. But once you do, pay attention, and start learning from the pros. It works for Warren and it will work for you.

CHAPTER 28

Move Up in Life

"It's better to hang out with people who are better than you. Pick out associates whose behavior is better than yours and you'll drift in that direction."

—WARREN BUFFETT

According to Warren, in the management of our personal lives, we are who we hang out with. Hanging out with a low-life will drag us down, while hanging out with a smart, educated person will draw us up.

Warren spent much of his time as a teenager at the racetrack, where he learned to calculate odds. Instead of falling into a life of gambling, however, he was able to put his knowledge of calculating probability to use in college and graduate school. He found mentors who were considerably older and wiser than he, who took an interest in him and steered him into the world of finance and investing. He moved up.

In Warren's early days of running an investment partnership, he cultivated friendships with Omaha's business elite, including Nick Newman, who took warehousing techniques developed during WWII and used them to create the modern supermarket chain; and Jack Ringwalt, founder of the National Indemnity Company, who introduced Warren to the concept of disciplined underwriting. Later in life, he spent time with Katharine Graham, owner of the *Washington Post,* and Bill Gates, founder of Microsoft. These friendships paid off for Warren over the years and gave him creative, successful business role models to emulate.

Warren's lesson here: We are who we associate with. Aim high in your associations and you will get to the top. Aim low and there is no telling how low you'll go.

CHAPTER 29

Manage "You" for Inflation

"The best asset during inflation is your own earning power. Anything you do to improve your own talents and make yourself more valuable will get paid off in terms of appropriate real purchasing power. If you do something well, whether you're a major league baseball player, or if you're a good assistant, whatever it may be, you are your best asset."

— WARREN BUFFETT

W arren says you should think of yourself as a business. Although you may not look like a business, or act like a business, you're a business, with an infinite ability to earn, and your greatest asset is yourself.

When you're young and inexperienced, your business doesn't make much money, but the more education and experience you acquire, the more your earning potential increases.

Education and experience are the two keys to getting your business up and running.

Whether you are an accountant or a rock star, everyone starts at the bottom and works their way up. Yes, Daddy may have opened a door or two, but the reality is that to get to the top and stay at the top, you must have the energy and the drive to excel at your chosen craft or profession.

Warren believes that you should take good care of your business, which means taking good care of your health and getting a good education. You should find ways to improve your earning potential and protect it from disaster. When it comes to staying ahead of inflation, nothing beats your potential to earn.

The more special your business is, the freer you are to raise prices. People in unique professions have always had the upper hand as an inflation hedge, because the lack of competition allows them to charge more for their services.

The rule here is simple: Each of us is an economic entity with great earning potential. If we take care of ourselves and get an education, our economic potential is infinite, and will not only keep up with inflation, it can even make us rich.

CHAPTER 30

Managing Personal Borrowing

"You can't borrow money at 18 or 20 percent and come out ahead. I can't—I'd go broke. So stay away from debt as much as possible. When you get an amount for a reasonable down payment, you find a home you like, buy it. But don't do it till you can handle it. And take on obligations you can handle, avoid the others."

—Warren Buffett

The world of retailing has gone from selling you a product to selling you the money to buy a product. The modern merchant makes money loaning consumers the money to make purchases. It used to be that merchants made their money on the mark-up of merchandise, but in the age of volume discounting and stiff competition, those margins have slowly eroded. But imagine if you could make money not only on the sale of the goods, but also by loaning the customer the money to make purchases. You get to cash in twice: when the consumer borrows the money, and when he spends it. When businesses learned that they could loan us money at 18 to 20 percent, they figured out very quickly that they could make more money by loaning money than they could by selling goods.

Credit card companies figured this out years ago. They finance the purchase of even the smallest items, and if you don't get your bill paid off in total or on time, they charge you outrageous interest. This is not just a good business; this is a great business and the merchants have followed. Modern furniture, appliance, and computer stores are all now banks in disguise. They would much rather finance your purchase of a new TV or refrigerator than allow you to pay in cash. In order to facilitate this money-making scheme, the modern merchant will offer you the product for no money down, and no payments for sixty days, as long as you sign the loan agreement.

Warren's advice is to play it safe and avoid any loan obligation that you can't comfortably handle. How safe? Warren paid $34,000 for his first house and he still lives in it. He drove a cheap car long after he was a millionaire. By being conservative with his money and not overspending, he accumulated a surplus to invest. He invested well and became superrich. He did this while others were busy accruing debt so that they could keep living in bigger and better houses and driving bigger and better cars. Think of this in terms of the tortoise and the hare. The hare piled on more and more debt so that he could live a faster and faster life, while the slow tortoise lived well below his means, investing the difference for his future. Along comes the recession and the fast-moving hare crashes and burns in an inferno of debt, while the debt-free tortoise keeps on going.

Remember: Borrowing less and saving more is the path to riches and to sleeping well at night. Borrowing more and saving less leads to wild times and bread lines.

In Closing

We want to thank you for taking this journey with us as we explored Warren Buffett's management secrets. For those of you who are interested in Warren Buffett's investment methods, may we recommend our other five books—*Buffettology, The Buffettology Workbook, The New Buffettology, The Tao of Warren Buffett,* and *Warren Buffett and the Interpretation of Financial Statements.*

For those of you with specific questions, please feel free to write (or contact) us directly at:

Marybuffettology@gmail.com
Davidbuffettology@gmail.com

It may take us a while to get back to you, but we assure you that your thoughts and ideas are very important to us, and we very much look forward to hearing from you.

Best wishes,
Mary Buffett and David Clark

Select Glossary of
Terms and Companies

Balance sheet: A summary of a company's assets, liabilities, and ownership equity as of a specific date, such as the end of its fiscal year. A balance sheet is often described as a snapshot of a company's financial condition on a single day within the year. There is no such thing as a balance sheet for a period of time. A balance sheet tells you how much you have and how much you owe. Subtract the two to see how much you are worth.

Benjamin Moore: A 127-year-old paint company that has sold the paint that is on just about every house in North America. Warren had Berkshire buy the company so he could add it to his collection of great businesses. Paint is a product that he can understand because it really doesn't change over time.

Berkshire Hathaway: A publicly traded textile manufacturer that Warren acquired control of in the early 1960s and that turned into a holding company for the expanding empire of companies he acquired partial and total control of over the next forty-five years.

Blue Chip Stamp: A trading-stamp company, which Warren had Berkshire acquire control of over a thirteen-year period, and which proved to be a losing investment, with sales going from $126 million in 1970 to $25,920 in 2006.

Blumpkin, Rose: Also known as "Mrs. B," a Russian immigrant and the founder of the Nebraska Furniture Mart. A professional who so loved her work that she stayed on with NFM until she was 103.

Boom-and-bust cycles: Economies go through periods of boom and bust. In a boom period the economy is growing and is usually marked by low unemployment and inflation and high interest rates. Bust periods are marked by a contracting economy, high unemployment, and low interest rates.

Borsheim's Fine Jewelry: An Omaha, Nebraska, jewelry store that Warren had Berkshire Hathaway acquire in 1989.

Brand-name product: A product name that you think of when you have a particular need, or that as Warren says, "owns a piece of your mind." Brand-name products can be gold mines in that they get preferential treatment when consumers go shopping.

Buffalo Evening News: A monopoly newspaper in Buffalo, New York, and one of the first companies that Berkshire acquired after Warren took control. When Warren acquired the *News,* Buffalo was a two-newspaper town, and neither made any money. The *Buffalo Evening News* went head-to-head with the competition and won. It has made Berkshire a lot of money.

Burlington Northern Santa Fe Railway or BNSF Railway: One of the four remaining U.S. transcontinental railways, which has only one competitor for western U.S. freight. Warren had Berkshire Hathaway acquire a large interest in the railway during the late 2000s.

Capital: Usually thought of as financial capital, which is money or a like substitute that is invested in a business. Can also mean capital goods, which are used to create goods and services that can be sold.

Capital needed for growth: Because businesses need capital to grow, this capital can be generated internally by selling goods and services, or it can be generated externally by borrowing it or selling shares in the company to investors.

Clayton Homes: The United States' largest manufacturer of manufactured homes. Was acquired by Berkshire Hathaway in 2003.

Coca-Cola Company: The world's largest beverage company, in which Warren had Berkshire invest in the late 1980s.

Compounding annual growth rate: The rate of a growth of pool of money on a yearly basis over a number of years. It compounds because the money it earns is added to the pool, so the pool keeps growing; the annual rate of growth is the compounding annual growth rate.

ConocoPhillips: An international energy corporation that Warren had Berkshire invest in during a rise in oil prices during the late 2000s. He admitted that he overpaid for his investment.

Cost of goods sold: The cost of inventory sold during a specific period, or the cost of obtaining raw goods and making finished products.

Debt: Borrowed money that can be used to leverage the earning power of a company's assets, but can become a detriment when the company can't make the interest payments to support the debt.

Delegate authority: When a senior manager gives a lower-level manager the power to act with the senior manager's authority.

Dempster Mills Manufacturing: A Nebraska-based windmill manufacturer in which Warren had his partnership invest in 1961 and eventually take control of. Dempster appeared to be a bargain purchase but turned out to be a low-return business, with lots of problems and the need for a change in management.

Durable competitive advantage: A competitive advantage that a company has in the marketplace that is "durable," meaning that it can be maintained over a long period of time. Warren believes that durable competitive advantage is the secret to successful long-term investing.

Erratic yearly earnings: Yearly earnings that are erratic, show no consistency, and usually indicate that the company in question lacks any kind of durable competitive advantage.

FlightSafety International Inc.: A company that trains professional airline pilots and is a subsidiary of Berkshire Hathaway.

Forest River: A U.S. manufacturer of recreational vehicle products that was acquired by Berkshire Hathaway in 2005.

Fruit of the Loom: An American manufacturer of cloth, primarily underwear, that was acquired by Warren's Berkshire Hathaway in 2002.

GEICO: An auto insurance company that caught Warren's eye when he was in his twenties and that he later on had Berkshire buy. Tony Nicely, who runs GEICO and has worked for the company since 1961, has no idea what he might do if he ever retires. (He really likes his job.)

Gross margin test: The percentage of total profit to sales. The higher the better. Companies with a durable competitive advantage tend to have high gross margins.

Gross profits: Gross profits on sales. Sales – Cost of Goods Sold = Gross Profit.

H&R Block: Fifty-year-old American tax preparation company with more than 22 million clients that Berkshire invested in during the late 1990s.

Helzberg Diamond Shops: A ninety-year-old national chain of jewelry stores that was acquired by Berkshire Hathaway in 1995.

High debt loads: Any amount of debt that will cause problems for a company over the economic ups and downs that will occur over the long term.

Highly competitive industry: Any industry in which companies are competing solely on the basis of the price of their products.

Income statement: Shows a company's income and expenses for a specific period of time. But note: Warren has discovered that a single year's income statement tells us very little, and that we need to check out five to ten years' worth of financial statements if we are really serious about finding out whether a company has a durable competitive advantage.

Inventory: A company's products that are either completed or in some stage of completion, and that will be sold to the company's customers.

Inventory turnover: A ratio used to show the number of times that a company sells its entire inventory during the year.

Johns Manville: An American corporation that manufactures insulation, roofing materials, and engineered products that was acquired by Berkshire Hathaway in 2001.

Johnson & Johnson: A worldwide American pharmaceutical, medical-devices, and consumer packaged-goods manufacturer that was founded in 1886. J & J is a company in which Warren's Berkshire Hathaway has acquired a substantial stake.

Jordan's Furniture: A ninety-year-old furniture retailer that dominates eastern Massachusetts and southern New Hampshire. The company was purchased by Berkshire Hathaway in 1999.

Kraft Foods: The largest food and beverage company in the United States and the second largest in the world. Berkshire Hathaway acquired 8 percent of the company in 2008.

Locus of control: Used in psychology to refer to the extent to which individuals believe that they can control events that affect them.

Long-term investor: An investor with a holding period of five or more years.

Lousy business economics: Business economics marked by low margins, lots of debt, declining sales, and erratic earnings.

Low-cost buyer: A buyer who can acquire goods at a cheaper price than his competitors.

McLane Company: Highly successful $30 billion supply-chain services company providing grocery and food-service supply-chain solutions for thousands of convenience stores, mass merchants, drugstores, and military locations, as well as thousands of chain restaurants throughout the United States. Was purchased by Berkshire Hathaway in 2003.

Merck & Company: One of the largest pharmaceutical companies in the world.

Microsoft: Multinational software company founded by Warren's friend Bill Gates.

MidAmerican Energy Holdings: A Berkshire subsidiary and the holding company for MidAmerican Energy Company, PacifiCorp, CE Electric UK, CalEnergy Generation, Kern River Gas Transmission Company, Northern Natural Gas Company, and HomeServices of America, Inc.

Moody's: Holding company for Moody's Investors Service, which performs financial research and analysis on commercial and government entities. The company also ranks the credit-worthiness of borrowers, using a standardized ratings scale. The company has a 40 percent share in the world credit-rating market. Warren has invested in the company several times during his career.

Multinational conglomerate: A company with operations in many different countries.

Nebraska Furniture Mart: A Berkshire Hathaway subsidiary, located in Omaha, Nebraska, that was started on a shoestring in the 1930s by Rose Blumpkin, a Russian immigrant. Possibly the largest single furniture store in the world, with the best margins. Mrs. B said her secret was in the buying: She bought in large quantities and always paid cash and owned her own building, which helped reduce her costs. Lower costs mean lower prices for customers, which enabled NFM to take a greater market share of the Omaha furniture business.

No/low debt companies: These are unique businesses, which generate so much money that there is little need to go into debt.

Owning a piece of the consumer's mind: The same as having a brand-name product: When the consumer wants to satisfy a particular need, he thinks of your product.

Philosopher's stone: A tool alchemists used to try to turn lead into gold. Something that Warren has been able to do with Wall Street's folly.

Profit margin: Net profit divided by revenue, then multiplied by 100 percent. A low-profit margin indicates a low margin of safety: There is higher risk that a decline in sales will erase profits and result in a net loss.

Recession: The name for a contraction of a nation's or industry's economy. During a recession, employment, investment spending, household income, business profits, and stock prices all fall. Warren has always used a recession as a buying opportunity for businesses and stocks.

Retool plant and equipment: When products have to change, companies have to retool their plants and equipment to make the newer products. This of course costs money to do, and reduces capital for acquisitions and other forms of business expansion. Warren has never been a big fan of companies that continuously have to retool their plants and equipment to stay competitive.

Revenue: Income that a business receives from its normal business activities. In the United Kingdom, revenue is referred to as turnover.

Right business: In Warren's world the right business is one that has a durable competitive advantage.

ServiceMaster: A privately held Fortune 500 company that provides various services to residences and firms. Brands operated by ServiceMaster include: TruGreen ChemLawn, Terminix, American Home Shield, Furniture Medic, AmeriSpec, ServiceMaster Clean, InStar Services Group, and Merry Maids.

Shareholders' Equity: The net worth of a business. Total assets – total liabilities = shareholders' equity.

Superior economics: The economics of a business, which shows high returns on shareholders' equity, above-average profit margins, and low debt-to-equity ratios.

Wal-Mart: The brand name for Wal-Mart Stores Inc., an American corporation that runs a large chain of discount department stores and is the world's largest public corporation by revenues.

Wells Fargo: Wells Fargo is the second largest U.S. bank in deposits, home mortgage servicing, and debit card transactions. In 2007 it was the only bank in the United States rated AAA by S&P, though its rating has since been lowered to AA—in light of the 2008 financial crisis. Berkshire owns 7.2 percent of Wells Fargo.

Wrigley: The brand name for Wrigley Gum, manufactured by the William Wrigley Jr. Company, which was founded on April 1, 1891, originally selling products such as soap and baking powder. In 1892, William Wrigley Jr., the company's founder, began offering chewing gum with each can of baking powder. The chewing gum grew to be more popular than the baking powder itself, and Wrigley's reoriented the company to produce the popular chewing gum. It now sells its products in more than 180 countries.

ACKNOWLEDGMENTS

Mary would like to thank . . .

Her wonderful daughters, Erica and Nicole Buffett, with love and respect. Her sister and confidante, Dorothy Manley. Her kindred spirit Maureen Thompson, for her creative influence. The first lady of class, Phyllis Bart, and her kind and scholarly husband, Peter. Jocelyn Skinner, who keeps our world turning and is the best friend anyone could have. And the prince and princess of all adventures, Richard Bangs and Laura Hubber. Gretchen Rollins, my muse and confidante, and trust that our screenplay will be as successful as our books. Of course, Kitty O'Keefe, my professor. And always my inspiration and son, to whom this book is dedicated, Sam Buffett-Haygood.

David would like to thank . . .

Kate and Dexter Clark for their love and never-ending patience. Sam Clark, Alexander Payne, Bob Eisenberg, Todd Simon, Steve Joy, Terry Rosenberg, Larry Bolding, Jon Jabenis, and Gerry Spence for their never-ending friendship. David would also like to thank Jeremy Utton and Tim Vick for both their friendship and their financial insight in these interesting times.

And a special thank-you from both Mary and David to the staff at Scribner and our wonderful editor, Roz Lippel.

INDEX

opportunities, 91, 109–11
orders, 83–87

PacifiCorp, 137
PepsiCo Inc., 6
performance-based pay, 53–54
per-share earnings test, 11–14
PetroChina, 72
Philip Morris, 6, 76
philosopher's stone, 47, 136
plants and equipment, retooling
    of, 4, 140
popular opinion, 31–32
praise, 61–62, 69, 71–73
Proctor & Gamble (P&G), 6
production, 63–64
products, unique, 5, 6–7
professions, 35–36
profit margin, 136
profits, 15–17, 45, 46
public relations, 46

Raff, Beryl, 57–59
recessions, 137
    of '09, 96, 97, 99
reputation, 63–66
research and development, 3
responsibility, 32–33
retooling, 4, 137
Revenue, 15, 16, 137
Ringwalt, Jack, 114–15, 118
Rosier, Grady, 22
Rosner, Benjamin, 46

salaries, 14, 53–54
salespeople, 37

Salomon Brothers, 103–4
Schwab, Charles, 61–62
Securities and Exchange
    Commission, 103
self-financing, 14
ServiceMaster, 7, 137–38
ServiceMaster Clean, 138
services, unique, 5, 7–8
shareholders' equity, 138
software, 17
Sokol, David, 68
stocks, buy-backs of, 12
subprime mortgages, 99, 100–101
Sudan, 72
superior economics, 3, 141
sycophants, 91, 107–8

tax-filing business, 7, 8
tech companies, 17
Terminix, 138
Treasury, U.S., 101, 103, 104
Treasury Bonds, 103, 104
TruGreen ChemLawn, 138
turnover, 140

Ueltschi, A. L., xiii—xiv, 40–41,
    80–81
underwriting, 115
United Airlines, Gross Profit
    Margin of, 17
USAir, 105
U.S. Steel Company, 61, 130
    Gross Profit Margin of, 17

victor vs. victim mentality, 31, 32–33
volume discounting, 121